ABOUT THE AUTHOR

Kayleigh Campbell finished her PhD at The University of Huddersfield in March 2022 and is a member of the Editorial Board for Grist Books. Her poems have appeared in *Rialto, Butcher's Dog, Stand Magazine* & *The High Window*; she was shortlisted for the Bridport Prize 2021. In 2019, her pamphlet *Keepsake* was published by Maytree Press.

www.kayleighcampbell.co.uk

Kayleigh Campbell
Matryoshka

VERVE
POETRY PRESS
BIRMINGHAM

PUBLISHED BY VERVE POETRY PRESS
https://vervepoetrypress.com
mail@vervepoetrypress.com

All rights reserved
© 2022 Kayleigh Campbell

The right of Kayleigh Campbell to be identified as author of this work has been asserted in accordance with section 77 of the Copyright, Designs and Patents Act 1988.

No part of this work may be reproduced, stored or transmitted in any form or by any means, graphic, electronic, recorded or mechanical, without the prior written permission of the publisher.

FIRST PUBLISHED MAR 2022

Printed and bound in the UK
by ImprintDigital, Exeter

ISBN: 978-1-913917-09-8

CONTENTS

Darling	9
Matryoshka	10
Departure	12
Lucienne	13
Exit wound	14
Ghosts	16
Loch	17
Devil's bridge	18
Insects	19
Bottled Goods	20
Three Sisters	21
Ariana Grande said god is a woman	23
A Poem for Lyudmila Petrusheskaya	24
Death of the cherry blossom	26
Exhibition	28
Saint Tatiana(s)	29
Dear Vera Shimunia	32
Writing playlist	33
Ode to Paris	37
Cemetery	39
Hallgrímskirkja	40
Two women at sea	41
Two women in a lighthouse	43
Summer in Reykjavik	44

Mollusc	45
Berlin	46
Martha	47
Slaughter	48
A gift	49
Lost	50
Flight	51
Drugs are not her thing	52
Piscine	53
Hare	54
Oksana	55
Lunar Eclipse	56
Stockholm	57
Tomorrow	59
Fontanelle	60
Stargazing	61
Girls on Holidays	62
Adrift	63
Locket	65
Summer in Krakow	66
Beached	67
A short French film	68
Tivoli	69
Swallows	70
Dear Katerina Marchenko	71
Bound	72

Acknowledgements

Matryoshka

Darling

after Anna Akhmatova

All that you are hangs by a thread —
tonight, tomorrow & always.

Whoever you are,
do not die young, but live dangerously.

Black is good for all occasions,
and the world is an endless funeral.

Matryoshka

A mother gathered her seven daughters
around the fireplace.
She poured each daughter a glass
of violet coloured champagne.
She watched as they sipped;
she smiled as they shrank
into little, wooden dolls.
She lined them up on the mantlepiece.

Every one of her visitors raved
how beautiful the dolls were,
how similar to her daughters.
They remind me of them whilst they
are away, travelling the world.
More visitors came from afar
to see the dolls.

The mother began to hate
that people loved them so.
Even the Mayor came knocking!
Now, there was no answer.
The Mayor peeked through
a window; inside the house

everything was as it should be.
A plate of biscuits on the table,
white roses.
The Mayor pressed an ear to the glass;
the house was spider quiet.

But one thing
had changed.
Above the fire
stood a single doll.

Wide, bright eyes,
wide, bright smile,
an emerald dress.

The seven
little dolls

nowhere in sight.

Departure

For Alexandra Dvornikova

She receives an envelope from Saint Petersburg.
Her mother is alarmed by this news —
surely it will be laced with poison!

Don't open it — her mother hovers at her side.
She uses her index finger to slice open
the envelope with the precision of a knife.

She gently removes the contents.
A postcard, with an image of a small, porcelain
hand; resting on the hand are three
death's-head hawkmoths.

See! says her mother —
A bad omen; poison, foreign!
She looks up and notices she is now standing
beneath deep green spruce trees.

Her mother is drowned out
by the sounds of the forest.
She looks down again; the hawkmoths
depart from her hand and she watches
their flight for as long as she can see.

She climbs a half-tree and sits atop it.
She takes out her notepad and some ink.
There is no malice here; only two young
women with wild imaginations.

Lucienne

remained at the cliff edge
her feet dangling above

      the Irish sea

longing for the tide
to return her lost   love

Exit wound

She sets the table —
two plates, two knives, two forks,
the good paisley tablecloth, tulips
in the best crystal vase.

The oven pings as the front door opens.
She hurries into the room, smiles.
Eyes flash across at the table

A plate shatters against the wall.
She watches as the shards scatter into chaos.
There is no sound anymore,

just raging arms, a moving mouth.
She stares at the debris;
the shards begin to move.

They move into formation.
They have become a woman's face,
pale and distorted.

The silence is broken by shouting.
She cannot hear the words
she can no longer see the face.

The tulips have bowed —
she picks them from the vase.
She pulls the tablecloth from the table,

cutlery clatters, the other plate cracks;
she drapes the table cloth over her shoulders.
She ducks from a fist.

She hurries out of the front door,
tulips in her hand,
paisley cape blowing in the breeze.

Ghosts

Everybody is prone to googling
their symptoms then diagnosing
themselves with Fibromyalgia
or Chronic Fatigue Syndrome
or Premenstrual Dysphoric Disorder.

They need to label things,
to understand why they can't sleep
on any random Tuesday.
Perhaps it is as simple as ghosts
haunting their restless, tender hours.

Loch

You look out across the darkness of it
and see no monster here, only a lone woman
swimming into the deep of it.
Something pulls behind her
but you can't see what it is.
Suddenly you are cold and damp;
swimming towards her.
You stop, breathless.
She stops and turns; she is featureless.
But still, you know her.
Below the surface is a cord,
floating between you.

Devil's bridge

Follow me,
tie your tongue, leave the words in the car.
I know you want to say them
but I need you to fill your lungs
with my apologies — breathe them in slowly.

Find me amongst birch, alder and aspen.
Help me grind myself into the soil,
so it replaces cuticles, seeps through pores.
Listen to the silence, revel in the breaking of it.

Water rushing over rocks, ledges, lost belongings.
Threaten to push me through tired rope
into rock pools and foam.
No, hold me;
we are only here for a day.

Insects

We spend our afternoons in the garden
passing the lethargic, post-nursery hours.
You wilt in the mid-July heatwave
and throw yourself on the ground, demanding milk.
It is gone in several gulps.
You lay still, your eyes slowly blinking.

Suddenly you crouch like a cat, face low
to the garden flags looking for insects.
At first with awe —
Ladybirds! Clover Mites! A beetle!
Then you spot an exhausted, nondescript fly
as it clings to a plastic toy in the paddling pool.

You watch it for a moment,
before dunking it below the surface.

Bottled Goods

After Sophie Van Llewyn

There is a kind girl
who offers what she can,
smiles and says nice things.
The girl apologises
for the faults of others.
When the sun goes down
she retreats to a room
filled with books and fairy lights.
On the shelf above her bed
is a row of miniature glass bottles
filled with glitter, dried flowers
and the shrunken bodies of those
who underestimated her,
soundlessly clawing on the glass.

Three Sisters

She can't sleep again —
even after a bedtime infusion
of camomile, valerian root and rose.
She scrolls through Apple news:

Alternative, quiet but beautiful hikes.

A meteor seen over Japan.

*A mother who aided the killing
of her six children is being released
from prison after half her term.*

Johnson, Starmer, Sturgeon.

Her eyes grow heavy from the bright
screen; a star amidst the dark.
They close on three Russian sisters.
An alternative Chekov plays behind her eyes.
Three sisters have carved their story
on apartment walls.
They scrape mucosa from their tongues
to erase the taste of the lump of skin
who is now slumped in the armchair.
They gather around ceremoniously
and puncture the sleeping, cold heart.

They listen to it deflate; she whispers
that she would do the same.
They stay still, watching life leave
the body that made them,
the body that ruined them.

Ariana Grande said god is a woman

Her sister asks her to bring a dog collar
and some ginger bitters.

Her sister stands facing the wall
and fixes them both a Moscow Mule.

Her sister starts to confess —
things she's heard before.

She lets her sister finish her drink,
tells her to find god or a therapist.

A Poem for Lyudmila Petrusheskaya

i.
There Once Lived a Woman Who Killed:
a baby a fly an abuser a mouse
a child a mother a sister a spouse
a dog a daisy a stranger a grouse
a friend a colleague a song & a louse.

ii.
There once lived a woman
who killed
herself
then buried her body.

iii.
There once lived a woman
who strangled her lover
with some tights
she wore for work the following day.

iv.
There once lived a woman who killed
accidentally.
One morning she needed some air
so she flung open her bedroom window
without even noticing the cat
perched on the ledge there.

v.
There is a woman losing sleep
thinking of her daughter's fate
as she grows with each passing season.

If the daughter turns out to be a killer -
a plant, a cat, a lover -
the mother is sure there'll be good reason.

Death of the cherry blossom

It is our house and it is not our house.
White patio doors; neat emerald grass.
I'm trying to save something; I can't see what it is.
You are in the living room, behind glass.
Our daughter is beside you, her face is blurred.
Suddenly there is nothing to save anymore.
It's your fault; my fist finds your face.
You tell me I'm insane.

Our daughter is somewhere else now.
A moment passes and I find myself in a forest clearing
surrounded by dandelions and nettles.
Amongst horse chestnuts is a single cherry blossom.
It is the same tree that bloomed in my parent's front garden
every year before my mother ordered the death of it.
I walk towards it; with each step the blossom
withers into lonely petals, bark falling like tears.

The sky is too blinding now, like driving in low winter sun.
I can no longer see, or feel around me.
I can hear the white noise of a heartbeat, soft breathing.
My legs give way like the breaking of twigs.
I open my eyes. You are next to me, snoring.
My face is wet and hot.
I walk towards our daughter's room;
I open the door like a plaster peeling from a wound.

Moonlight slithers in through the blind.
A quick look: the garden is our garden.
Swing set, old deck chairs, a row of conifers.
In the middle of emerald grass,
a scattering of blossom like ashes.

Exhibition

I will write to Natalia Deprina
and ask her to photograph me
as one of her girls in the garden of the dead.
Let gypsy moths be ornaments
on my bone china skin.

I will write to Lieke van der Vorst
and ask her to pencil me into a boat
full of sunflowers or etch me into a coral reef
surrounded by mandarin fish.

I will write to Melodie Stacey
and ask her to nestle me into a cabin
beneath the northern lights,
surrounded by snow and memory.

I will ask Raija Jonkinen
to embroider the outline of my body
with flax and fill it with thistles,
daises and lavender.

I will write to Mariachiara Di Giorgio
and ask her to paint me as I climb
into the belly of a blue whale.

Saint Tatiana(s)

i.

Saint Tatiana was good to the bone,
which was exposed when they cut
off parts of her broken body.
Virtue ran through her blood;
she prayed for those who tore
her skin with hot iron.
They took her hair, then finally her head.
In her absence lays a wreath of tulips.

Saint Tatiana was a star waltzing
through Moscow.
People gasped at her shimmer,
grasped at her flicker.
An artist for the people of Russia.
No money, only stardust
and her Anna Karenina dress.
The cranes flew into the night
as she closed her eyes,
exited stage left.

Saint Tatiana was a natural leader.
Sources say she was the most
beautiful of the royal sisters,
and her mother's favourite.
Romances with soldiers —
though she was married to Russia.
She embroidered a red cross
on her heart. She read the bible
every evening until one night
a bullet entered the back of her head,
leaving a hole like a small,
misplaced halo.

Sweet, little Saint Tatiana.
Only four years into her life
shadowed by destruction.
The woman who brought her
into the world, was the woman
who took her from it.

ii.

The sonographer laughed —
I think we can see what it is!
She stared at the screen.
She too saw it; she stared at it
until her eyes could see only
darkness.

She would not give birth
to her Saint Tatiana.
She would not able to atone,
to live again through a daughter.

Dear Vera Shimunia

embroider me a star
scattered night sky

with my body sewn
into it as a constellation

so I can hang myself
and the universe

on the kitchen wall

or embroider me a field
of sunflowers

sew every centre
as a black hole

so I can face the sunshine
and then disappear

into dreaming

Writing playlist

i.
Tacocat really speak to me
when they say they hate the weekend.
We wish the week away
for that Friday night feeling.
Saturday means nothing.
And I fucking hate Sundays.

ii.
I'm the heroine of this tale
I don't want to be saved.
My blood type is T
          [Trauma]
Regina says no one has it all
and it will be alright. alright, alright.
Everything is dreamlike.
I don't need to be saved because
I'm the heroine of this tale.

iii.
Laura said she loved you but maybe
she was wrong. She couldn't love
in this new romantic way.
I am a romanticist. I love Budapest
and pink skies in the mornings.
But I can't love in that new romantic
way. My personality type is avoidant.

iv.
I'm the girl in yellow
I'm feeling high on serotonin.
I laid in a field of daisies
and dandelions who've lost
the sense of time without their clocks.
I've painted my house in borrowed light
and I'm feeling high as a cloud
way above all the noise.

v.
My watch pings telling me *Breathe*.
I'm inhaling and exhaling just fine
through the lungs of Florence.
One day I knew the dog days would be over.
Life exploded like a party popper;
streams of the rainbow.

vi.
The world is burning.
Boney M are singing
Ra Ra Rasputin
Lover of the Russian Queen on Radio One
and I'm craving a mint Aero.
They say it'll be a girl
if you want sugar, spice and all things nice.

vii.
Their words can't bring me down
Like Lana I've been raised from the dead.

I have good customer service skills.
I'm very organised.

I think I'd make a good necromancer —
I'd bring the all the best girls back.

viii.
The world in a Camera Obscura.
Full of strangers and lonely people.
A tiny shadow walking through the chaos.
I knew they had the morning sky on their mind.
I knew then they were my darling;
finally someone of my kind.

ix.
Every morning I have a Japanese breakfast.
I don't regret my cruel thoughts.
I'm always searching for goodness.
The bad people seem to always win,
the selfish people seem to shout the loudest.
I'll keep on searching for goodness
like finding the toy in cereal box.

x.
Lykke Li is right
I fall fast so steep low
everything is made of sandpaper
I can't feel at home in this world
I never have
Lykke Li is right
I'm no longer woman
    just a   single   ray of   light

Ode to Paris

The morning of the flight
she had googled *painless ways to die*.
She bookmarked an article
about the inhalation of helium.
She packed a navy polka-dot dress,
cherry lipstick and propranolol.
Off she went to the city of love
with the lover she despised.

The taxi stopped outside the hotel;
in that instant, she knew.
There would be no Paris Syndrome.
Rather, she fell in love immediately,
with the Arc de Triomphe roundabout,
Darjeeling in the Café de Flore,
the île de la Cité florists.

After three days —
which included a proposal,
an argument over a Métro stop
and sleeping with the light on —
she said *Au Revoir* to Paris.

Returning home and opening the door
she looked at the ring on her finger;
there would be no wedding,
for she no longer existed.

The article is gathering dust.
She is currently living in Saint Germain.
Paris is a cliché as much as it is beauty.
To her it was a defibrillator.

Cemetery

There are those who cannot fathom
how a woman could find walking
amongst the dead peaceful.

There are those who cannot fathom
why a *pretty young woman*
would walk through a cemetery
alone at night, by choice.

There are those who cannot fathom
how she could not fear the danger
in the graveyard shadows.
Why she walks further into the dark
as a lone, almost shooting star.

Hallgrímskirkja

She looked upwards like an ant
looking at a crumb of glorious cake.
She walked nimbly beneath the stained-glass
archway; inside her ribs vibrated
with the organ pipes.
She thought not of god, but of the poet.
The poet's church.

Concrete columns infused with
basalt, echoes of the Passion Hymns.
The lift took her to the top of the tower,
as if being elevated to heaven.
She could almost touch the clouds.

The city below was a patchwork, rooftop quilt
of currant red, banana yellow, sea green.
As she was on the roof of a church,
she forgave herself of any current sins
and took a picture for Instagram.
In the distance she spotted Cafe Babalu —
forgiveness had made her hungry for cake.

Two women at sea

i.

Eventide has fallen, the North Sea has settled.
Two women sit in the cabin of a small fishing boat.
They are drinking scotch from tea cups,
dipping bread in vegetable broth.
Lucia breaks the silence and begins to talk
of all her unborn children again.
I had names for them all.
Lucia tops up her cup, looks to the crescent moon.
Celeste sips her scotch, *I am with child*
she says as she drags her spoon through the broth.
Lucia lights a cigarette — *You'll be a good mother, won't you.*
I think so, says Celeste.
Lucia blows out smoke — *We'll see, won't we.*

ii.

A month has passed, Lucia and Celeste
are still surrounded by sea, the salted air.

Celeste is weak with sickness and longing
to be grounded by the stillness of land.
She finds comfort in the gentle kicks.

Lucia smokes less than she did a month ago
and sings quietly to herself in the mornings.

iii.

Time has been lost somewhere at sea
when the boat finally docks.
Lucia is alone — no, she has a small bundle
nestled against to her chest.
There is no body nor burial but there is a wake.
People dressed in black gather around
as Lucia recalls the peculiar and tragic events.

The child was a surprise —
Celeste simply emerged from the cabin one morning,
she never made a sound.
I was busy gathering fish.
Lucia sipped scotch from a cup, paused.
She was sad — she hid this from me too, poor darling.
That evening I was tending to the child whilst she got some air.
I never saw her again.
I found a note tucked into the child's blanket,
it said:

I know you'll be a good mother.

Two women in a lighthouse

You chop   the head off a trout.

I regurgitate   last night's dream.

You stand   in a puddle of blood.

I lick   salt from the rocks.

You invite   your ghosts for supper.

I scream   into the easterly wind.

You make   a necklace from trout bones.

I sleep   wrapped in seaweed.

You climb   inside an oyster.

The sun sets.   The sun rises.

Summer in Reykjavik

    she laid in the hotel bed
        painting her lover
            with the rare evening light

    they fell asleep as the sun set
        just before midnight
            a bewitching palette of pinks
        and oranges

    she woke to the summer sunrise
        resting gently on her healing skin

Mollusc

A woman once googled if snails
feel the pain of love.

Researchers say no, as snails
cannot process emotional information.

The woman searched for an empty
snail shell; she found one and crawled inside.

Her heart remained broken.

Berlin

Your face was so typically sad:
drooping mouth
vacant eyes
increased blood flow
to otherwise pale cheeks.

All the more illuminated
in the too-bright Chinese
restaurant in Charlottenburg.
Koi in ponds, a green dragon
looming above our table.

No, that was me,
just my reflection
in the mirrored ceiling.

Martha

In the evenings Martha wanders around
her village as a mischievous cat —
if a window is open, in she goes.
She jumps into cots with sleeping babies
tickles their faces with her whiskers.
She kneads her damp, muddy paws
into fresh white bedding.
She releases mice in pantries.
Tonight she sneaks into a bathroom,
Behind the frosted glass she can see
blurry strong thighs, a fuzz of brown hair.
She purrs with excitement.
She taps her right paw three times;
She sheds her fur and is female-form.
Naked, she steps into the shower.
Beneath two closed eyes she kisses the soapy lips
the eyes pop open —
in a flash she's feline again, out the window
and off into the starry night.

Slaughter

After Anna Akhmatova

Women have always been slaughtered.
They are not led to believe that they too
can wield the knife.

She learnt that she could hack away
the bits of memory she did not want.
She learnt she could cut people off like limbs.

She learnt the art of hanging oneself
in the abattoir, hollowed
before turning without looking back,
walking away newly formed.

A gift

The first time the cat left her a mouse,
stiff and intact apart from two small,
bloodied holes, on the doorstop
she felt a wave of elation.

She'd heard about this —
they leave you gifts.
Science suggests this is the act
of a natural mother, a teacher.
Her theory is love.

Last Wednesday a tiny thing
in the foetal position on the doorstep.
Yesterday, another one
amongst the snowdrops.
She shovelled it onto the dustpan
and studied it for a minute,
then flopped it into the sack of leaves.

Each time a new one appears
she ponders how cruel nature can be
yet how lovely it is to receive a gift.
As her stomach grows she uses an app
which tells you how big the foetus is,
week eleven is the size of a fig.
She imagines week twelve as a tiny mouse,
in the foetal position.

Lost

Madeleines
are one of the reasons she wants to live.
They are better than sex, like most things;
they give her tongue a warm bath.

But every time she puts one to her lips
she remembers lost girls, the ones
who cannot taste the comfort from petite sponges.

If only the memory of lost girls could be poured
into rows of shell-shaped depressions and rise
in the oven, then given fresh to those in need of the missing.

Flight

When her children are cutting shapes
from felt, making happy Easter cards
and her other-half sits at a desk
by a picture of her and the children smiling,
her breasts are pressed against
the full-length mirror
fogged with her lover's breath.
Later, she packs a holdall
with thrown together outfits.
She trips on a small bunny by the door.
She scribbles words full of ink
but no meaning on a post-it note,
then leaves.

Drugs are not her thing

She knows a girl who took a pill then started hissing/
at the mirror/screaming *I'm a vampire*/drugs are not her thing/
she's sure they make you happy/make you fucking love the
stranger in the toilets/but other times its/anxious/confused /
paranoid/panicked/she knows she'd be submerged/in the
depth of psychosis/and not become a hissing halloween
vampire/ but Elizabeth Bathory/smothering girls/with honey/
and garnishing them with ants.

Piscine

As children our bodies in bloom
would emerge
like brittle water-nymphs
peeking out over the edge
of the pool
at the bare-chested
sunbathing women.

How fascinated we were
by strangers' breasts.
How excited we became
for the future.
Beneath the water
we pulled at each other's
bikini strings, giggling.

Hare

    she was wandering
        through the lowland meadow
    when a hare crossed her path
        it hurried into a small opening
    into the intricate wetland
        looking back at her swiftly
    then disappearing
        she followed the hare
    crawling
        the dirt seeping through her skin
    hearing her own breath
        and the earth
    crunching under her limbs
        when she emerged and stretched
    she found herself
        in a purple heathland
    somewhere
        she had forgotten the hare
    until she saw it crouched
        in the heather
    then she too shrunk
        into her wilderness

Oksana

i.

There once was a woman who walked away.
She walked until she found the forest;
she walked until night surrounded her.
Beneath the moon her mouth began to howl.
She pulled away her clothes before cutting out
her womb, cradling it until the morning.

ii.

Scattered clothes were returned to her body,
which were found by police in the forest.
They could not find her uterus.
The police looked for the prints of a monster.
There were only size three, petite footprints.
They concluded that grief had taken place —

they say you can still hear the howling.

Lunar Eclipse

For Wang Zhenyi

She stared at the triangle between her legs,
the darker tip of it like a snow-covered mountain top.

She lifted her foot from the water
and suspended, curled it into a skin-covered moon.

She lifted her right hand as Zhenyi
might have, scrunched it into an earth-fist.

She held her left hand up, palm flat, fingers
outstretched into a pygmy sun and paused:

nothing and everything changed.
She let her limbs go limp once again.

Stockholm

In the Fotografiska I meandered through
Nygårds Karin Bengtsson's Untold Stories.
A woman, laid on the floor
with her head buried in the seat of a sofa.
A woman, sat at a small wooden desk
with her head buried in a cardboard box.
A woman bending forwards her head buried
in a field of yellow tulips.

A woman, in a leather waistcoat
auburn tones in her hair,
behind a criss-cross of metal.
A hand on her shoulder, a hand on her arm.
Her head and another, angled diagonally
in the shape of a heart.
I take a picture of this story.

I think of her often, if it was real love or not.
If it was a secret love, a goodbye or a hello.
If it was comfort over the death of a pet.
If she didn't want to be there.
If she didn't want them to leave.

In the early mornings, when sleep
has already left before I wanted it go,
I curl up beneath the desk
my head buried into my chest.
I think of them.
I think of the woman sat at the wooden desk,
the woman with her head in the cardboard box.
The woman behind the criss-cross of metal
All of us, untold stories.

Tomorrow

After Natalya Gorbanevskaya

If I had my way, then tomorrow
you'd not even find a trace of me,

a flicker of what I was
or of what I might become.

But for now I am here —
incandescent.

Fontanelle

Delicate, round.
Not a perfect circle
like they teach you in school.
Lumpy in places, fuzzy fur on top.
A fragile peach,
two days before the use-by date.
In the palm of her hand:
easy to squash, fleshy.
Juice spilling though her fingers.

Stargazing

In the salmon pink painted waiting room
she reads a pamphlet about diabetes.

In the box room through door
the nurse collects her blood in a vacutainer
and asks *is this decision supported?*

Yes & no,
like everything in this fucking world.

In a another room beyond that
she is asked *do you want to look?*
At the miniature milky way on the screen.

Years from now she might carry a star
but now she's no divine mother, only a telescope.

Girls on Holidays

Her sisters, in crop tops and anklets,
met transitory beaus in the pool bar.

Later they climbed over the balcony, ran
across spiky, jade grass dodging sprinklers.

Laying on the apartment sofa bed,
her prepubescent body dewy under the sheet,

she looked at the window and dreamed
of climbing out into the wilderness of

brightly coloured cocktails and Umbro bucket hats,
dizzy from the idea of being grown up

like the moths
       around the balcony light.

Adrift

For Alexandra Dvornikova

When I open my eyes I am looking up
at the bright, grey sky.

I can feel something heavy on my chest,
feel the weight down to my shins —

I do not look down at it.
I turn my head to the right.

I can see panels of wood.
I turn my head to the left.

I can see panels of wood.
I focus on the grain.

I feel then that I am moving, gently.
I can smell a faint note of sulphur.

I raise my arm, hold my right hand
in front my face — it is not a hand,

but a paw. It is not my arm but a limb
covered in pecan-brown fur.

I look down now at the small body
resting on mine. Honey-blonde hair,

a sunflower clasped in small hands.
I look back up at the bright, grey sky.

I let my eyes close; we drift.

Locket

People say her heart is made of gold.
A pendant to a chain, whispering
look at me; I'm so sweet, so loving.

The heart may be made of gold
and it may never rust nor corrode
but if you open it up you will not find
a tiny picture of her beloved, only,

nothing at all.

Summer in Krakow

She is sipping from a small glass of Krupnik.
She is alone, writing postcards to all her lovers.
She leans back, takes off her sunglasses.
She leaves one hundred zloty as a tip,
slips away into late afternoon.

Early the following morning,
she returns to the table,
her hair in a loose bun, still wet.
She sits down, orders a small glass of Krupnik.
I left my postcards on the table.
The waiter smiles warmly at her;
I post them for you.

They spend the morning together;
the waiter talks of childhood,
she hums to nondescript cafe music.
They make Szarlotka cocktails,
sweet like apple cake.

She licks her lips —
honey, jasmine and caramel.
She kisses the waiter abruptly,
then slips off into the late afternoon.

Beached

I cover my body in St Ives apricot scrub
not because I want to be blemish free
but so I can be a shell in the sand,
iridescent beneath the sun.

I want to be walked over
not because I believe I am nothing
but so I can exist anonymously,
to be different kind of atoms.

I want the option of being treasured
or discarded; to drift with the tide.
To be still but change with time.
To keep the company with the sea.

A short French film

[Early Summer in Caudéran.
A girl in a lavender skater dress enters the bakery
below her apartment, leaving with a cannelé
and fresh orange juice.
She walks to Parc Bordelais and sits down
under an oak tree, inhaling the scent of rosemary
and fennel drifting from the nearby herb garden.
She begins to read *A Beast in Paradise* by Cécile Coulon.
After a few pages she is interrupted.]

A handsome stranger, not a local:

>That book looks interesting -
>care to tell me what it's about?

Girl:
>Oui c'est et non merci.

Tivoli

She had a breakdown so she went to Copenhagen
where she had a second breakdown.

She had dinner at Nyhavn with people dressed as vikings
she returned to the hotel on a train with no driver.

The next day she had melancholia for lunch;
she saw a polar bear pacing up and down.

That evening she saw murmurations of bikes
and a Louis Vuitton solar system.

In the Gardens, she ate at an American diner
overhearing conversations about someone's infidelity.

For dessert she studied her convex body
and the concave bodies of strangers in fairground mirrors

that are truer to life than those that hang in bathrooms
or stand at the end of beds, suggesting everything is in order.

Swallows

It was early June when she sat
in the small decked garden
with a small body resting in her arms,
a small mouth attached to her breast.

The swallows had nested in the eaves.
They were darting outwards into the cloudless
sky and inwards again with lunch.

She placed the now sleeping body
gently down in the Moses basket
in the shade of the house.

She felt herself ascending, weightless
away from the garden.
She glanced below, promising
she'd begin her descent sometime,

                                        soon.

Dear Katerina Marchenko

embroider me new eyes
sapphire blue or burnt amber

my own have seen nothing
and enough

I can cut it carefully from its hoop
then cut out my old eyes

placing the embroidery in their place
to see the world differently, freshly

Bound

After Marina Tsvetaeva

Whimsical sisters,
where are we bound?

Where do the bad girls go?
The bad girls who aren't really bad.
They were just in the wrong place
at the wrong time or under duress
it was just a mistake, it's the wrong data
in the spreadsheet.
Deconstruct their skeleton
examine the bones
drill into the maxilla
drill into the metacarpals
they are not made of evil —

Take a breath, slow down.
All girls are hell-bound.

Miss Murder, Miss Cadaver.
Monarchs and maidens.
Lost girls, joyful girls, wicked girls.
Save themselves for marriage girls
save themselves from marriage girls.

We will all walk through
an orchard of apple trees,
in the moonlight, knowing we are bound
for the eternal darkness
to be stars lightyears beneath the ground.

ACKNOWLEDGEMENTS

Firstly, I would like to thank Steve Ely as his guidance throughout this project has been invaluable. It is because of Steve that I write the way I do and his module Liberating Poetic Chaos which I studied in my final year of university was in many ways life-changing. I would also like to thank Michael Stewart, Sarah Falcus and James Underwood at The University of Huddersfield for their advice and support. A huge thank you to Stuart Bartholomew and Verve Poetry Press for seeing something special nestled in *Matryoshka*. I would like to give thanks to Jon and the late Elaine Glover at Stand Magazine, where I volunteered in my earlier days of writing poetry. Their kindness and dedication to the craft of poetry were comforting and inspiring. Thank you to the wonderful publications where some of these poems have appeared. Thank you to all my 'poetry' and 'creative' friends for encouragement and support, especially Jack McLean and Julie Irigaray. Lastly, thank you endlessly to my dearest Joe.

Some of these poems or versions of these poems featured in publications prior to the release of *Matryoshka*, details as follows:

'Fontanelle' featured in Issue 12 of *Butcher's Dog* magazine November 2019.
'Beached' featured on *Anthropocene* in December 2020.
'Dear Vera Shimunia' and 'Lunar Eclipse' featured on *Fragmented Voices* in April 2021.
'Death of the Cherry Blossom' featured in *Stand Issue 230, Volume 19 Number 2* June- July 2021.
'Devil's Bridge' featured on *Ink, Sweat and Tears* in November 2019.
'Stargazing' was shortlisted for the 2021 Bridport Prize.
'Two women at sea' and 'Mollusc' featured in *The Rialto Issue 97*, Winter 2021.

ABOUT VERVE POETRY PRESS

Verve Poetry Press is a quite new and already prize-winning press that focused initially on meeting a local need in Birmingham - a need for the vibrant poetry scene here in Brum to find a way to present itself to the poetry world via publication. Co-founded by Stuart Bartholomew and Amerah Saleh, it now publishes poets from all corners of the UK - poets that speak to the city's varied and energetic qualities and will contribute to its many poetic stories.

Added to this is a colourful pamphlet series, many featuring poets who have performed at our sister festival - and a poetry show series which captures the magic of longer poetry performance pieces by festival alumni such as Polarbear, Matt Abbott and Imogen Stirling.

The press has been voted Most Innovative Publisher at the Saboteur Awards, and has won the Publisher's Award for Poetry Pamphlets at the Michael Marks Awards.

Like the festival, we strive to think about poetry in inclusive ways and embrace the multiplicity of approaches towards this glorious art.

www.vervepoetrypress.com
@VervePoetryPres
mail@vervepoetrypress.com